Foley

Published by Methuen 2001

1 3 5 7 9 10 8 6 4 2

First published in Great Britain in 2001 by
Methuen Publishing Limited
215 Vauxhall Bridge Road,
London SW1V 1EJ

Methuen Publishing Limited Reg. No. 3543167

A CIP catalogue record is available from the British Library

ISBN 0 413 77172 5

Typeset by SX Composing DTP, Rayleigh, Essex
Printed and bound in Great Britain by
Cox & Wyman Ltd, Reading, Berkshire

# Foley.

**THE CORN EXCHANGE**
**PRESENTS ANDREW BENNETT IN A NEW PLAY BY MICHAEL WEST**

# THE CORN EXCHANGE

In 1995, after having spent a few years in Dublin teaching, performing and giving workshops in **Commedia dell'Arte**, Annie Ryan spotted on the quays a crumbling Georgian facade with "The Corn Exchange" written on its rusting sign.

"Corn" was the word used at New Crime — the company with whom she worked in Chicago — to describe a certain kind of theatre: theatre that would work its actors like dogs, but do anything for a cheap gag; theatre that would make its audience laugh and cry at the same time. It described a kind of wild irreverence within a strict and respected structure. It was the kernel of Commedia dell'Arte, and the basis of New Crime. The notion of "exchanging corn" — sharing this way of working with other people and mixing it up with other forms of theatre practice which share that sense of structure and play — that seemed the very reason for making theatre in the first place. And here it was on a building. It seemed the perfect name for a theatre company. **The Corn Exchange** was born.

The starting point was this renegade version of Commedia dell'Arte from Chicago, and the exchange involved marrying the style with other performance disciplines to see what happens. The work so far has branched into three different, but overlapping areas: Commedia dell'Arte treatments of American classics, devised work through the strange and wonderful CAR SHOW, and work by Michael West, including A PLAY ON TWO CHAIRS, THE SEAGULL, and FOLEY.

TONY FLYNN IN *COMMEDIA DELL'ARTE IMAGE*. PHOTOGRAPH BY AMELIA STEIN

ANDREW BENNETT, CLARA SIMPSON AND ROBERT PRICE IN *THE SEAGULL*. PHOTOGRAPH BY PAUL McCARTHY

ROBERT PRICE, ANNIE RYAN AND CLARA SIMPSON IN *BIG BAD WOOLF*. PHOTOGRAPH BY PAUL McCARTHY

THE CORN EXCHANGE PRODUCTIONS BY **MICHAEL WEST**

# Foley.
by Michael West

**BEST NEW PLAY / BEST ACTOR 2000**
Jocelyn Clarke, The Sunday Tribune

**SIMPLY SUPERB**
Helen Meany, The Irish Times

**WEST'S PLAY IS A SPLENDIDLY CRAFTED ACT OF SELF-CONSCIOUSNESS**
Nelson Pressley, The Washington Post

**IT IS ONE OF THE BEST AND MOST ORIGINAL PIECES OF NEW IRISH DRAMATIC WRITING TO EMERGE IN SEVERAL YEARS**
Karen Fricker, Irish Theatre Magazine

# The Seagull
by Anton Chekhov, in a new translation by Michael West

**A MATURE INTERPRETATION OF CHEKHOV... A GLITTERING NEW VERSION**
Jocelyn Clarke, The Sunday Tribune

**THE WHOLE THING WORKS SPLENDIDLY, THE PLAY RETAINS ITS INTEGRITY ... THE CAST DO AN EXEMPLARY JOB, TRUE TO THE DIRECTOR'S INTENTIONS, AND ULTIMATELY FAITHFUL TO CHEKHOV'S SPIRIT**
Emer O'Kelly, Sunday Independent

**THE CORN EXCHANGE HAS DESERVEDLY GARNERED PLAUDITS FOR ITS INVENTIVE AND ICONOCLASTIC CANON OF WORK TO DATE AND THE DELICIOUSLY IRREVERENT TONE OF THE SEAGULL GOES SOME WAY TO JUSTIFYING THIS REPUTATION**
Declan Burke, The Sunday Times

# A Play On Two Chairs
by Michael West

**A JOYOUSLY INTELLIGENT, ENTERTAINING AND SEXY PIECE OF THEATRE**
Jocelyn Clarke, The Sunday Tribune

**WITTY, FAST AND SURPRISING...INTELLIGENT AND HIGH ON HUMOUR.  SEXY, WITTY AND VERY SHARP**
Grania McFadden, Belfast Telegraph

**EDGILY FUNNY, SOMETIMES DISTURBING...SUPERB ...PROVOCATIVE AND BRITTLE INTELLIGENCE**
Declan Hassett, The Examiner

**FIERY AND SEXY...TERRIFICALLY LITHE AND EXPRESSIVE...CRACKLING EROTIC ENERGY**
Joyce McMillan, The Scotsman

# Car Show (4 SHOWS IN 4 CARS)
Winner of the Cultural Inspiration Award 1998
Winner of the Special Judges Award, Irish Times/ESB Theatre Awards 1998
No.1 in Susanna Clapp's Top Ten Theatrical Events of 2000 for The Observer

**INGENIOUS, VIVID, IMPORTANT WORK... NEXT YEAR SOMEONE SHOULD FIND IT A PARKING PLACE AT THE LONDON INTERNATIONAL FESTIVAL OF THEATRE**
Susannah Clapp,  The Observer

**THEATRE AT ITS BEST**
Gerry Colgan, The Irish Times

**GET IN LANE**
Helen Meany, The Irish Times

**BUCKLE UP, THIS IS WHAT FRINGE FESTIVALS ARE ALL ABOUT...ONE OF THE MOST INTENSE THEATRICAL EXPERIENCES EVER**
Sophie Gorman, Irish Independent

**THE CORN EXCHANGE HAVE TRULY OUTDONE THEMSELVES WITH CAR SHOW...A TREAT**
Karen Fricker, The Sunday Tribune

**THE BEST PIECE OF THEATRE TO BE FOUND IN DUBLIN FOR MONTHS...ASTONISHING AFFIRMATION OF THE POSSIBILITIES OF THEATRE, SETTING A STANDARD WHICH NOTHING IN THE MAIN FESTIVAL CAME CLOSE TO ACHIEVING.**
Michael Ross, The Sunday Times

ANDREW BENNETT (FOLEY), PHOTOGRAPH BY PAUL McCARTHY

ANNA HEALY AND ANDREW BENNETT IN CAR SHOW. PHOTOGRAPH BY PAUL McCARTHY

ELIZABETH KUTI AND ROBERT PRICE IN A PLAY ON TWO CHAIRS. PHOTOGRAPH BY PAUL McCARTHY

# The Corn Exchange Commedia dell'Arte Productions

**ASTONISHING PHYSICAL THEATRE WHICH PROMISE SO MUCH FROM THE CORN EXCHANGE IN FUTURE**
Jocelyn Clarke, Sunday Tribune

**FIRST-RATE...BRILLIANTLY EXPLORED THEATRE'S CAPACITY TO SHOCK**
Karen Fricker, Sunday Tribune

**ELECTRIC ENSEMBLE PLAYING...LAUGHTER SPIKED WITH PAINFUL RECOGNITION**
Helen Meany, The Irish Times

**NEW AND RADICAL PIECE OF THEATRE — AND ONE WHICH IS UNIQUELY THE CORN EXCHANGE'S OWN**
Jocelyn Clarke, The Sunday Tribune

**THE EFFECT IS ELECTRIC: TREMBLING ON THE KNIFE-EDGE OF HILARITY AND HORROR**
Mic Moroney, The Sunday TimeS

# THE CORN EXCHANGE

**ARTISTIC DIRECTOR: ANNIE RYAN   COMPANY MANAGER: JENNY HUSTON**

**BOARD OF DIRECTORS:** Siobhan Colgan, Aileen Corkery, Brendan Courtney, Victor Merriman, Maura O'Keeffe (secretary), Gaby Smyth, Morleigh Steinberg.

**THANK YOU:** THE ARTS COUNCIL \ THE BELL TABLE ARTS CENTRE \ THE CULTURAL RELATIONS COMMITTEE
DUBLIN CORPORATION \ STENA LINES \ MARGARET WARREN and THE BOATHOUSE \ MARY COLL
PAUL MCCARTHY \ ÉAMON LITTLE \ TARA FURLONG \ MORLEIGH STEINBERG \ DES KENNY \ THE GATE
PJ BRADY OF PERIOD DESIGN \ ANTHONY CUDLIPP of RENAISSANCE
THE TYRONE GUTHRIE CENTRE at ANNAGHMAKERRIG \ MAURA O'KEEFFE \ FELICITY O'BRIEN \ LISA MAHONY

## FREE MAILING LIST

| | |
|---|---|
| Post: | Mailing List, The Corn Exchange, 43/44 Temple Bar, Bar, Dublin 2, Ireland |
| Telephone: | +353(0)1 679 6444   Fax:   +353(0)1 679 6284 |
| Email: | info@cornexchange.ie   Url:   www.cornexchange.ie |

The Corn Exchange Theatre Company Limited. Company Registration no. 335369

Cultural Relations Committee
Department of Foreign Affairs
Ireland

# Foley.

A NEW PLAY BY **MICHAEL WEST**

ACTED BY **ANDREW BENNETT**   DIRECTED BY **ANNIE RYAN**
MUSIC BY **VINCENT DOHERTY**   LIGHTING DESIGNED BY **EAMON FOX**
SET DESIGN BY **AMANDA HOGAN**   PRODUCTION MANAGEMENT BY **LEE DAVIS**
PRODUCED BY **JENNY HUSTON**   MARKETING & P.R. BY **JENNY HUSTON**
GRAPHIC DESIGN & LANDSCAPE PHOTOGRAPHY BY **NIALL SWEENEY** FOR **PONY**
PHOTOGRAPH OF ANDREW BENNETT BY **PAUL McCARTHY**

FOLEY WAS ORIGINALLY CO-COMMISSIONED AND CO-PRODUCED FOR THE UNFRINGED FESTIVAL AT THE BELLTABLE ARTS CENTRE, LIMERICK IN FEBRUARY 2000

## ANDREW BENNETT

Stage work includes THE SPANISH TRAGEDY and THE WHITE DEVIL for Loose Canon; WHAT WHERE, Heiner Muller's MEDEA and EARLY MORNING with Bedrock; WE OURSELVES for Passion Machine; GOOD EVENING MR. COLLINS, THE MARRIAGE OF FIGARO, SOUR GRAPES, THE ELECTROCUTION OF CHILDREN, TARRY FLYNN, THE RIVALS, ST. JOAN, THE MAP MAKER'S SORROW, THE HOUSE, TRANSLATIONS and TARTUFFE for the National Theatre. Film and TV work includes QUICKFIX (Eamon Little), ALASKA (Michael West), THE GENERAL (John Boorman), THE AMBASSADOR, MULBERRY (Howard Gibbons), DAVID COPPERFIELD (David Medak), ANGELA'S ASHES (Alan Parker), TRI SCEAL (Owen McPolin), PATHS TO FREEDOM (Ian FitzGibbon).

He first met Annie and Michael in 1993. Since then he has taken part in extensive Commedia dell'Arte workshops and one-off improvisational pieces with The Corn Exchange, as well as working on Commedia dell'Arte productions of American Classics, CAR SHOW, THE SEAGULL and FOLEY.

## LEE DAVIS

This is Lee's first time working with the Corn Exchange, but he has been a life long fan! He is the company Production Manager and lighting designer with Bedrock productions in Dublin, and has worked for Fishamble, Loose Canon and Opera Theatre Company amongst others. Lee won the Sunday Tribune best lighting design award 2000 for his design of Bedrock's 'Wideboy Gospel'. He has also designed lights for the bands Interference, The Eggs, Igloo, The Nualas and Mundy. Lee is the technical director for the Dublin Fringe Festival.

## VINCENT DOHERTY

FOLEY is Vincent's fifth show with The Corn Exchange, having scored all of the work to date. He was also a technical designer for CAR SHOW. Other plays include the productions QUAY WEST and NIGHT JUST BEFORE THE FOREST for Bedrock and THREE DAYS OF RAIN for Rough Magic. Most recently Vincent composed music for Read Co's PLAY ABOUT MY DAD.

## EAMON FOX

Eamon graduated from Trinity College Dublin obtaining a degree in Drama and Theatre Studies. He has worked as a freelance lighting designer and production manager since. He has re-lit extensively for Barabbas the Company and for Cois Ceim Dance theatre where he also was the production manager on their last two pieces. Recent Lighting designs include BOXES for Cois Ceim, DIE FLEDERMAUS for Co-opera, ROMEO and JULIET, EDUCATING RITA, both for the Pavillion Theatre and ALICE IN WONDERLAND for the Civic Theatre.

## AMANDA HOGAN

Amanda Hogan, a graduate of 1991 from The Samuel Beckett Centre, TCD, has spent the last nine years working both in Ireland and abroad. Amanda has worked on diverse projects, designing exhibition space, interiors, furniture, costume and set. She is currently living and working freelance as a designer in Dublin.

## JENNY HUSTON

A graduate of University College Dublin's Arts Administration Studies 1998, Jenny has worked in various producing and administrative roles within the Arts and Entertainment sectors including; voice-over management, Radio and Television production. Since starting as Company Manager with The Corn Exchange in July 2000 she has produced the Dublin Fringe Festival production of FOLEY, the 2001 FOLEY Irish Tour, FOLEY at the Traverse Theatre, for the Edinburgh Fringe Festival 2001 and CAR SHOW 3 for Draíocht, Dublin.

## ANNIE RYAN

Born and raised in Chicago, Annie moved to Ireland in 1992. She was trained in the Piven Theatre Workshop, Chicago and received a BFA from NYU. She was a member of John Cusack's Commedia dell'Arte-turned-movie company, New Crime for three years. She has acted extensively in theatre and film in the US and Ireland. In 1995 she founded The Corn Exchange where she directed all of the work to date including Chekhov's THE SEAGULL translated by Michael West and CAR SHOW (winner of the Irish Times/ESB Judges Award 1999 and listed first in The Observer's Top Ten UK Theatrical Events in 2000).

## MICHAEL WEST

Michael West's most recent play is DEATH AND THE PLOUGHMAN, a translation of a 15th century Bohemian text. It was produced by Project Arts Centre and the Comédie de Reims. Other work for The Corn Exchange includes a translation of THE SEAGULL, A PLAY ON TWO CHAIRS, and CAR SHOW. In collaboration with TEAM he has written two plays for children: FOREST MAN and JACK FELL DOWN. Other work includes versions of THE MARRIAGE OF FIGARO (Abbey); TARTUFFE (Gate); Molière's DON JUAN and THE TENDER TRAP (an adaptation of La Double Inconstance by Marivaux), both for Pigsback. He has also translated or adapted work by Arrabal, de Musset, Bely and Brecht. Other plays include MONKEY, SARDINES, SNOW, THE QUIRK ESTATE, and a piece for radio, THE DEATH OF NATURALISM. FOLEY won The Sunday Tribune award for Best New Play 2000.

**THE CORN EXCHANGE**

# Foley

Michael West

**Methuen Drama**

# Foreword

In the bar of a theatre in France, a woman I had never met before told me a story about her first trip to Scotland. Why she told me this story I have no idea. I was part of an Irish contingent attending a festival in Reims, and perhaps because they were stirring up a particularly giddy atmosphere that evening she was swayed by the Celtic association.

She told me that she had taken her new lover on their first trip away together to the wild and desolate landscapes of the Highlands. She was driving the car when, without warning, she stopped and got out.

'What are you doing?' asked her lover, 'It's freezing.'

She walked away from the car and stood facing into the wilderness.

He called out to her to come back to the car, but she remained where she was, her coat flapping in the wind.

And then she heard it: a faint drumming far away. It got louder and louder. Until over the hill came a group of horses, galloping at full speed towards her. In the lead was a white stallion. They came nearer and nearer, with no sign of stopping. She stretched out her arms. The horses kept running. The turfy ground was vibrating from their hooves and their breath was alarmingly loud.

They pulled up sharply some yards away from her. The white horse was looking at her the whole time. The other horses nodded their heads, sniffed the air and wheeled away. Only the white horse remained.

He came up to her and bowed his head. His nostrils flared, he pawed the turf with his hoof. She looked into his eyes and didn't break his gaze. She had been in a serious relationship that had ended badly. She had not known if she would ever find true love. Her affair with the man in the car had just started. She was wondering if he was the one, if there was such a thing as The One, if she would ever meet her other half.

And here he was in the shape of half a ton of feral Scottish stallion.

The white horse stepped up to her and nosed her face and neck. He was drooling foamy suds and the breath from his nostrils was hot and wet. He was shaking his head and nuzzling her hair, her outstretched arms, her breasts, her ribs, her thighs and stomach. He was butting her with his muzzle and drenching her with spume. It was freezing. The wind was blowing. Her lover was calling her from relative safety behind the car to leave the animal alone.

And then it was over. The white horse raised his head high and stepped back. He swung his head once more over her, as if inhaling the last lingering fragrance, then he turned and trotted off, picking up speed until he was once more at full gallop, and disappeared over the horizon.

She was left standing there, devastated. She began to wail. Her friend tried to comfort her, but she was beyond consolation. She wept for twenty minutes and was unable to drive away, even when she had clambered back into the car. She wept for her lost love, the only true love she would ever know; she wept for him to return, she wept out of the knowledge he was gone to her and would never return.

Over the next few days she and her companion fought. She was miserable at the prospect of never seeing her horse again. At first he was understanding, but then he became irritated and tried to make light of it. She called him jealous, and he was. For her it was a tragic encounter, a doomed love affair. For him it was a catharsis – and something straight out of a tourist brochure.

On their return to France they decided to get married. He learnt to drive. She took up dressage. 'But they are just horses.'

I clutched my glass and nodded in agreement. There followed a long awkward silence.

I had just finished the first draft of *Foley* the week before, and myself, Andrew Bennett and Annie Ryan had begun work on the text only a few days previously. In fact as I stood there I could see them chatting and laughing on the far side of the room.

When I began writing it, the piece had at its centre an encounter with a horse. In truth the encounter with the horse was the only concrete thing I knew about it.

I had a notion that it would be about a man who loved Protestant funerals. This was coupled with an image of a foley artist on stage, banging doors and making noises with coconuts.

The funerals were subsumed into the background to the play; the image of the crazy man slamming doors turned out to be a dimly remembered nightmare about badly built sets. Mercifully you have been spared this anxiety dream. There are no doors, and all references to synching sounds and actions have slipped away, unheeded and unlamented. And I wound up with a title.

The encounter with the horse, however, remained at the heart of the thing, and as we worked on it for the first time we knew that the piece would stand or fall by those sections. But there was the nagging doubt, as it were, whether anyone would believe the premise of a life-changing epiphany with a large quadruped.

You dream of these moments of synchronicity, but when they actually happen you're not sure if you dreamt of them with longing or dread. Do they confer on you the blessing of coincidence, or the charge of poor imitation?

For that matter, I have no idea if the French woman's story of the white horse was the dense psychodrama she related to me, or a rich dramatisation of feeding a carrot to a Shetland pony.

I don't think I care. That night in France a small champagne-coloured window opened on the world we were looking to create. And selfish as it was, I felt a thrill that was not entirely due to the effects of bubbles going to my head.

Michael West
Dublin, July 2001

*Foley* premiered at the Belltable Arts Centre, Limerick, on 3 February 2000, toured throughout Ireland and was subsequently performed at the Traverse Theatre, Edinburgh, in August 2001.

**Foley**   Andrew Bennett

*Directed by* Annie Ryan
*Designed by* Amanda Hogan
*Lighting by* Eamon Fox and Morleigh Steinberg
*Music by* Vincent Doherty
*Stage management by* Tara Furlong

Thanks to:

Jenny Huston and the Corn Exchange; Mary Coll and Siobhan Colgan, both formerly of the Belltable, Limerick; Margaret Warren and the Boathouse, Castletownshend, Co. Cork; the Tyrone Guthrie Centre at Annaghmakerrig, Co. Monaghan; the Arts Club, Dublin; Des Kenny and Tara Furlong; Lyric FM, Amanda Hogan, Morleigh Steinberg and Eamon Fox; the beast that was Vinandes, Laurence Browne, George Dawson, Tom Murphy, Tracey Elliston and the Arts Council/An Comhairle Ealaíonn.

Finally, I owe a great debt to Vincent Doherty, both for his beautiful score and his constant presence; equally to Andrew Bennett, Annie Ryan and Thomas Henry, who was late for the opening but still on time.

*A table and chair.*

**Foley** *enters.*

I used to associate solitude with self-improvement and self-knowledge; it was linked in my mind with the idea of travel, of bravely setting off into the unknown, defiant and independent.

Solitude, like travel, was a choice you made to affirm your identity. It was a chance to take stock of your life by moving away from it for a while, or better, it was a chance to leave your life behind.

And god, how I wanted to. God, how I wanted to.

Even so, yesterday I found an old pair of shoes. In a bag, under the bed. There are holes in the soles and they are dusty and creased. Still, they're considerably better than the ones I must have replaced them with.

I'm wearing them now.

So you see, the past always catches up with you. No matter how far you go, how much solitude you can bear.

And now I'm reduced to this, solo excursions in a hostile world – like the hunter-gatherers we are supposed to have improved on.

At the end of the Ice Age, the last Ice Age, there were only 10,000 or so of us around. Ten thousand humans. Ten thousand souls. You could conceivably have met them all, us all – all of humanity. Imagine that. It's like Johnson's boast (I think it was Johnson) of having read all the novels written in English. And if you were my father, you could conceivably have gone to all of their funerals.

I don't know when his obsession with funerals started but it seemed at one point as if he was determined to bury every last Protestant in the country. It certainly seemed feasible – the Church of Ireland is a satisfyingly small community and dying all the time.

Not that she would think that a bad thing.

But I digress. My father. Yes.

My father's two grand passions were his land and his beloved funerals. Although he attended the latter with a diligence all too often absent from his labours with the former. The former. That sounds like a bad accent.

You couldn't quite call him a farmer. At least it conjures up the wrong image in my mind. No.

Gentleman farmer. It's a ridiculous phrase, but it does at least convey something of his inherent contradictions and aspirations.

He loved Castleowen, but I think he expected the fields to farm themselves, in a polite and orderly fashion, according to his inconstant whim.

He used to attribute to the land a form of primitive intelligence, an earthy wit, if you like. I can hear him still – 'To keep land you must enter into a dialogue with the forces of nature, a conversation. You can no more force it to your bidding than you can gravity or magnetism. You may as well try and float the apples back into the trees.' He would survey his fields and inform anyone listening, 'The land knows what it wants.'

The land knows what it wants. My god, then it had very low expectations. Merely to thwart my father was sufficient. Funny, I don't know why it and I weren't better acquainted. We had that in common at least.

*

The one exception to this laissez-faire version of cultivation was the orchard, the pride of the family estate.

It had been planted over two hundred years ago and had been the key attraction for my mother in marrying my father. She loved gardening, my mother. She had fabulously blunt hands. Tough-skinned and leathery. Her fingers looked like they had been pruned. Pollarded would be more the word, and recognizes the considerable contribution made to their knuckly look by arthritis. I'm mixing things up again, that was later.

Anyway, it became her garden. The crumbling greenhouses, the loganberries, the spiky quince. But most of all it was the apple trees. Beauty of Bath. McIntosh. Can't remember the other one. Cooker . . . something.

She was always out there, picking lichen off the branches, pruning the stunted trees still further. Lamenting that they only produced every second year, and every second year when they did condescend to ripen, letting the apples rot on the tree or fester in the grass. Food for the wasps.

O we picked them as well. We'd have wicker baskets of the things around the house, drying out on newspapers, for what I don't know, we never ate them. Rows upon rows in the spare bedrooms, like little shrunken heads, an entire conquered tribe sitting glumly in an abandoned trophy room.

The orchard had had a special role in the destiny of our family ever since it had forced my great-uncle to emigrate. He must have been great-great-uncle. He was obsessed with people stealing the apples.

Of course there was probably something to be jealous of back then. But come September, the locals used to shin over the crumbling wall with some old sacks and rob the orchard during the night.

It drove him mad. The family story goes that if they had simply asked during daylight hours then they would have been welcome to collect the windfalls.

I doubt it.

Anyway, the fact they never asked meant it was mutually understood they were not welcome, and I'm sure that was the point of the whole exercise.

Each year the locals couldn't wait for autumn.

And autumn came. The trees were groaning with fruit. And one night my great-uncle decided to keep watch. With a servant. And a gun.

I imagine one of those blunderbuss trumpet affairs, but that is being a little disingenuous. It was probably an army rifle.

They waited and waited.

And sure enough, over the wall came softly stealing a few of the unwashed apple thieves.

Anyway, my great-uncle shot a poacher, but the papers said he shot a Catholic and he was finished. The authorities invited him to evade arrest by running off to Australia. Or perhaps he had the wit to run off of his own accord.

A lasting legacy of this episode is that my father used always refer to Catholics as poachers.

*

It is strange how events in one's life – chickenpox, adolescence, your wife leaving you – should be so hard to reconstruct.

Perhaps reconstruct is the wrong word. Evoke. Re-evoke.

One can appeal to the senses, the primitive triggers of smell, taste, sound . . . And if you get these right, whole worlds can open up.

Nothing reminds me of Castleowen like the caw-caw of the rooks in the stand of elms. Unbelievable racket. Mary, our cook, used to feed them (why I don't know). She'd stand outside the kitchen on the grass and fling crusts in the air.

And the sight of them wheeling in the skies at dusk.

They used to build their nests in the chimneys as well. When the rage took him, my father would fire a shotgun up the flue to clear them out. 'Bastard crows.'

Yet these memories are unstable. They ebb and flow with the pull of Castleowen, of family, of identity. Images beget other images and you find yourself miles away from the truth.

But there are some events that stand outside the pull of association, that are isolated . . . *transcendent*.

There is a particular walk I have in mind. I went there the day she left.

Or more correctly. The day she did not come back.

You see, there's no sound for that.

Perhaps I am telling you all this to see if there is some clue, something I missed, that will explain to me her departure.

No. That would be too easy. Because I know why she left.

The fact it came as something of a surprise to me then, comes as something of a surprise to me now, as I contemplate it. Yet when it finally happened – although we had both known all along our parting was inevitable – when she actually left me, never to return, I was surprised. I was . . . speechless. My mother would have approved.

*

I went out for a walk. In those days the nights were dark, and I walked down by the river. I walked upstream, I suppose, inland. But it felt like you were actually going downhill, the land sloping away from you, from the sea, the natural order and consequences of things. But of course you weren't.

I doubt if I can convey the thrill of those solitary walks. You were walking, you were walking quite quickly, but it felt like you weren't going anywhere, that you were treading water almost, that you were, somehow, present – that's it, that you were still, and at the centre of the world, and it was the world that was moving, almost at your behest.

Am I going too fast? Forgive me.

She always used to say I spoke too fast, by which she meant in her rather approximate style of nagging that I thought too fast, my speed of speaking being almost unimaginably constant, and in either of two modes: silence or lecturing. As she called it. Cunt.

So. Off with a spring in my step, through the streets, down some anonymous quay, fine night, hops in the air – by which I mean the smell of hops, although I apologize, hops in the air is a rather silly phrase and somewhat beneath me. Walking for miles. Out of town. Buildings giving way to trees. Fields now behind walls rather than lots, walls turning slowly into hedges, and paths into verges, and the occasional glimpse of tractor tracks heading off to wherever their parallel business might be.

And coming one night, late, to a large rolling . . . pasture, would be the word for it. Pasture. Trees standing singly. Moonlight.

And a wooden gate in the hedgerow, the white hawthorn blossom brightening the bushes to either side.

And there in the moonlight, the smell of a horse.

The smell of horse dung actually, but it was a sweet surprise all the same. I could hear the horse breathe. That is, I could hear him before I saw him. And I could smell him before I heard him.

And there he was. He looked up and came towards me, walking full on, as if he expected me. He was grey. Dapple grey, but I couldn't see if that was because of the light, or . . . well it's all because of the light in the end.

Do you know, when a horse is walking towards you like that, his head nodding, and his hindquarters hidden, you could almost believe in centaurs.

Although they've the wrong head . . . Scrap that.

What I recall is the sound of four hooves on turfy ground, but only seeing the front two, so the hidden back hooves hitting the sods were like grassy echoes. It was the most eloquent sight.

He came up . . .

I assume it was a he, but do you know, I've no idea if he was. I'm sure I checked.

He came up quite quickly and halted abruptly some three yards off. He wanted . . . that's too venal. He was hoping . . . too pathetic. He was . . . curious, to see if I had brought him something, an offering. Which I hadn't. So I reached for a handful of long, and presumably not particularly delicious damp grass – the dew was rising and my feet were soaked. I took care to do this slowly so as not to alarm him.

The sound of his breath and the tearing of a clump of grass.

Once I proffered the wet handful, he took the four or five steps (which sounded out eight or ten times, the grassy echo, the grassy echo) and reached his muzzle toward me. The smell of his breath was exhilarating, and the sound of the air moving though his nostrils was one of the most captivating sounds I have ever heard. I could feel it on my inner wrists and fingers. I remembered to open my fist as I turned it – a beautiful gesture of thanksgiving. I opened my fist as he got close to the roots, and then, O delight, I felt his furry lips on my palm.

We contemplated each other in a way that would have been unknown to my wife. Regard without rancour, without pity, without accusation. Regard is a wonderful word.

And then he turned and ran off. Bolted. The gallumph gallumph over the uneven ground, the tail flashing.

O I don't know much about horses, don't even like the animals particularly, but I knew and liked this fellow. He was quite small. Twelve hands. Is that small? Small to medium was what he was. Medium . . . rare.

*

My father used to ride a horse to church. He didn't have to.
It was his fashion and his indulgence. The rest of us walked
or took the car. Or didn't go. But that was later. My father
liked to set off early and ride to St Bartholomew's the back
way, over the fields.

One morning the horse arrived at church without him. It
was so used to that Sunday run through the fields it knew
where to go. It turned up sometime during the Creed, and,
reins dangling, browsed on the vivid grass of the burial plots
until the blessing.

I can still see the empty saddle.

It's peculiar, you often see a saddled horse without a rider,
but usually because someone is about to get on, or has just
got off. But to see Claudius all dressed up – that was his
name . . . It was like seeing a car driving itself to town. It
was if he had saddled himself on his own, and had come to
church of his own accord because he was a good Protestant.

He loved that horse.

He called him Claudius, in honour of the Roman emperor
who so loved his horse he made him a senator, and I
suppose that tells you as much about my father as about the
horse . . .

Caligula. That was Caligula. Why did he call him Claudius?

Gone.

Anyway, he was a fine brown horse with black,
whatdoyoucallit, fetlocks, no, shanks, and a black mane and
tail, and we weren't allowed go near him by my father on
pain of death. And there he was eating the grass in the
family plot, saddled but riderless, in breach of the natural
order – there was something almost indecent about it. Like
seeing my father naked.

We eventually found him in a ditch – that part of him that
was still there, at any rate. He had fallen head first and
fractured his skull. The earth to which he had attributed a

form of primitive intelligence had, by violent exchange, now appropriated his, and in its place had left a groggy earthy sod.

I sometimes think we might as well have flung in a few handfuls of his beloved earth and let him lie there. Scant difference it would have made.

In any case there was justice in his fall. Or if not justice, poetry. For his fall joined together his passions – his horse, gravity, funerals and his land. And as he lay, witless in a ditch on the fringes of his estate, contemplating the changeable sky, he was closer than at any time in his life to the epitome of an Irish gentleman he so wished to be remembered as.

*

*A church bell tolls.*

The strict certainties of God.

Of morning prayer at any rate.

The strict certainties of the Reverend Flemming and the horsehair peeping out of the hard church cushions.

I got into trouble with Mr Carson the warden for plucking out small handfuls and dropping them over the balcony as parishioners were leaving, letting them fall through the Protestant air like wisps of pubic hair that had to be brushed off their disgruntled shoulders. (As if they had been overexuberant in their procreation.)

I spent many hours in that church, thinking, dozing. It's funny, at the time it seemed to consist of unremitting tedium, but I recall St Bartholomew's now with fondness. The pale sunlight occasionally streaming in the windows, the distinctive yowl of my great-aunt Hilda during the hymns. A meaningless hubbub of adult voices, akin to hearing your parents discuss matters over Sunday lunch when you were under the table.

And it was in that church I first saw the girl I knew I would marry.

Long black hair, a white coat or jacket with ivory buttons, ivory skin, and a little upturned nose.

She must have been about eight.

I saw her from the balcony, from above and behind, like I was her guardian angel, sent to watch over her. I was only a boy at the time, but I was struck with the revelation – the word is not too apocalyptic – that we were destined to be wed. If she would only look up.

If she would look up *now*.

If she would not look up.

She looked up!

What was her name? An . . . geline. Angela. Too obvious.

Gone.

Gone.

I don't know what happened to her. Why didn't I go up and talk to her? Was I doomed to thwart my destiny even at that age? Or perhaps that way was not chosen for me.

Chosen by me. For me. By me. Do you choose your life?

Or is it chosen for you? This is a very fine conundrum: How to reconcile the doctrine of free will with the doctrine of predestination? It has exercised finer theological minds than mine.

The only way I can conceive of it is that we are free to choose, and we are always wrong.

That would explain my wife.

And the fact I became a Catholic.

These two . . . things are forever bound up with each other. Which is more than can be said for me and her.

It started because she wanted one of her churches to house the happy event – the wedding, that is – and I thought: My parents, they will be mortified, but understanding. But if I could confound their understanding . . .

So I converted. I gave back the soup. I became a poacher.

Once the deed was done, the much-lauded difference between the religions seemed to amount to a few cases of standing instead of sitting, and remaining silent as opposed to speaking – with an extremely ecumenical sharing of uncomfortable benches and unbearable songs. I was also a couple of extra holidays to the good.

I can say nothing honest about the sanctimonious posturings of either since I was an arch-hypocrite in both.

Anyway, they said they believed me when I said I believed them, so fair enough. That's faith.

It's true that I found all the trappings in what she called the Old Church (but I called my New) rather vulgar. Candles, confession, statues, poor old gullible women, the horrid paintings.

That said, I found such trappings vulgar, but innocuous. After all, it is hardly a new observation that there are some tatty things in the world, and that includes both my wife and the Church of Rome.

In fact I got a mild frisson at their vulgarity. To me it was proof of my difference, proof that I had done something drastic, extreme and solitary. I was communing among the wafers and genuflections with myself and my . . . soul. In fact, becoming a Catholic was the most Protestant thing I ever did.

My taste for inversion and glibness disgusts me.

My poor parents. I confounded them all right. They were hurt because I would not talk to them about it, would not let them mention it. They tried to understand; I would not let them.

I was never rude to them – couldn't be rude to them. But I wanted them to suffer. If you don't understand me, perhaps you have never been taught the point of manners.

It was certainly something alien to my wife. God, she had no control.

I don't know what she thought was going to happen – that my mother and father would convert also? I laugh, but she was possibly that stupid. She would sit in the front room scowling as my mother cut her another thin slice of cake and topped up her chilled cup of tea. My wife, among alien corn.

My poor wife. All I wanted was to make a gesture. All she wanted was the house.

It was almost too much for me, to see her naked greed. She couldn't help herself, but everything she was handed, ate off, hung her coat from, she was reluctant to part with.

For some reason the piano attracted her particular attention. It was probably the pure uselessness of the thing that marked it out and shone like a beacon in the heathen night. I don't remember anyone playing it, any of us, ever, and she certainly hadn't a note in her head. Perhaps that was the attraction: we hadn't sullied it, and she could *learn*.

Our grand piano.

Baby grand. I must not exaggerate our heritage.

It must have been my mother's. And one day it would be hers.

*

The fields around the house were and always had been the subject of feverish debate. What do we do with them?

They had names that showed the spirit of invention that lives in the heart of our countryside. The Boggy field. The Lime field. The Six Acres. The Nine Acres.

My father tried many and various things. Grazing, tillage –
beets one year, I remember – a bit of forestry (total disaster).
He even raised a herd of dairy cattle for several years when
I was small, before they succumbed to TB – a loss that led
him to devote much of his spare time to the extermination
of badgers, to the considerable chagrin of the authorities.

'We've been killing things on this land for over three
hundred years. Those little grey shits owe me thirty-four
Jersey cows.'

Once my father and two of the McGettigans (the surly
hands he was upon occasion forced to hire) were out in
these fields when they saw smoke. So they walked up the hill
in order to see where exactly it was coming from, and it was
coming from our house!

And he and the men ran through the fields (the Boggy, the
Lime and the Six Acres). Mary, the cook, was wailing out
the back – 'I had an accident with the potatoes.' The
chimney in the kitchen had caught; a nest had fallen in and
was smouldering away. ('Bastard crows.') Smoke was
everywhere.

They shouted to see if there was anybody upstairs, and had
anybody been sent for, was the fire brigade coming? My
father and the men stormed inside and started rescuing the
furniture, picking up tables and chairs, beds, clocks, just
ferrying the stuff out on to the lawn.

They'd removed almost everything – everything except for
the baby grand piano beloved of my wife.

Just then there was a roar, the fire was picking up, the
pantry was about to go, and once it did the wooden back
stairs were next and the whole house would be up in flames.

So nothing for it, my father and the two McGettigans, in to
the drawing room, the three of them, one at each corner of
the piano and hup, they carried it out the front door, down
the granite steps, across the gravel and planted it on the

grass of the lawn. The fire brigade came and put out the fire and the house was safe.

I came home from school and thought we were moving.

I never realized we had so much stuff. There were things I didn't recognize, things I'd never seen before.

How strange it looked deprived of its natural habitat – naked, vulnerable, rather shabby. And what struck me most was that these things, these belongings – there was no natural law keeping them inside the house. They didn't necessarily belong, inside or outside, to anyone or anything.

And while the tables, pictures, cabinets languished on the lawn, inside, while I walked from room to empty room, amid the smell of scorched wood and paint, inside, the very house seemed to know this too, that its hold over them had been broken. Everywhere I looked, Castleowen was an acrid picture of loss. The carpets and walls bore the hallmarks, the outlines of their absences – like missing photographs.

It took an age to get everything back inside, but the pièce de résistance was the grand piano, so beloved of my wife, which had slowly sunk up to its ankles in the soft turf of the lawn.

In the end it took eight men an hour and a half to cajole and carry it back into the drawing room where it sat, unplayed, for eternity, for my wife to admire.

Maybe it was my first inspiration, an inkling of escape from a doomed and claustrophobic world.

An ivory tinkling inkling. (I'm being frivolous.)

He cut me out of his will.

I had renounced them. So he disowned me. No piano. No Castleowen.

I was without inheritance.

I was free.

I owned the things I stood up in, and no more. My clothes, my shoes . . . My shoes . . . A walk.

I was telling you about a walk. About the horse.

*

So. A few nights after she left I found myself retracing my steps. Streets, hops in the air (apology), quay, etc, etc.

I settled into the measured boredom of my walk, feeling in my pocket the tidy knot of an apple for my esteemed friend in the country. Aha, my horse, my horse. The hawthorn, the scent of flowering countryside, the must of dung and the gate, the beautiful wooden gate. And . . .

He wasn't there.

There were a pair of dun-coloured nags, a mother and foal, some way off. I called out for him. Not having a name I called him Centaur. I called and called.

I was . . . deprived of my adventure. There's always a punishment for wanting something. I walked for miles until my legs ached behind the knees. I took a bite out of the apple. It was bitter and I threw it at some rocks. I felt humiliated.

No that's not it. *She* wasn't there. A mare. I'm sure of it. I'm sure I checked. She wasn't there.

This is all going wrong. I'm forgetting . . . No I'm remembering too many things all at once.

First principles, first principles.

*

A distant cousin on my mother's side either was related to, or married, some explorer of the Antarctic or the Arctic, I forget. Or perhaps the Passage. Immaterial. Cold, wet, lost, ate his boots, bored with life after that and drank himself to death dreaming of barren wastes.

He suffered frostbite, too. His fingertips were blackened and I believe his toes were mostly missing. If you could have seen his feet. I don't imagine they were a pleasant sight.

A nurse, or my distant cousin, or aunt, whoever it was, had to change the dressings daily. Or at least however often you need to do such a thing. It's not like he was going anywhere.

And no doubt there they lurked at the end of his socks – little blunt black toes, festering like blighted potatoes in the bottom of a sack.

I mention this merely because of a curious relationship in my family regarding their own extremities – one of casual regard, carelessness even, of . . . critical detachment. Toes. Fingers. Earlobes. Distant cousins. Children. Me. My birth, for example.

You would have thought there would be, if not pleasure, then at least curiosity . . .

I cannot think of a word decorous and muted enough to do justice to their silently nodding heads. Faint civility, perhaps. You would have thought there would be faint civility enough to greet the knowledge of successful procreation, that some successfully scattered seed had made it into the world. Proof of having gone forth and multiplied.

In any case, I was not named for three months. Which does not inspire you with a sense of welcome.

In the end they called me by the same name as my father, they gave me his name.

It can hardly have taken three months and a whole gestation period to come up with nothing at all.

My mother and father were cousins – indeed that relationship seems to describe their common lot far better than man and wife, or whatever you say nowadays. Anyway, cousins. An archaeological vestige of something done between other people some time in the past.

But it would be wrong to suggest that there was no
happiness in their lives together. There wasn't. But it would
be wrong to infer it was because they were cousins.

After all, I was not related to my wife, at least not before I
married her, and we managed to be perfectly miserable
without any other excuse.

O there may have been a happy time, god forbid. It almost
turns my stomach to think of it.

They hardly spoke – certainly without the presence of
another in the room I can only conjecture a silent hush.
With someone there, me for example, they would
occasionally speak about the other, or about themselves,
referring at some point to the other, in the form: 'Of course,
your mother wouldn't agree, would you, you old neuhm
neuhm neuhm.' Or, 'Your father would probably not
approve, would you, dear, would you approve of that, you
wouldn't, he wouldn't.'

With regard to congress of the other kind – well, I don't
know when it stopped, if it stopped before the fall, but up till
then he was most punctilious in his duties in that respect.

It seemed to be Sunday evenings as a rule. I'm sure it was
Sundays. A few drinks after dinner, then up to her four-
poster bedroom. (Separate rooms.) The boots on the stairs,
the pounding on the door, the muffled cry of surprise. And
my mother – for it was she – bore it with stoical grace and
no little decorum. She would always retire in time for him to
fortify himself – too early might induce overfortification,
which would render her citadel impregnable, and too late
might leave him short of the required zeal.

One night . . . I must have been about – Who cares? Under
ten. I woke, or hadn't slept, or hadn't eaten, or had been
sent to bed without food, it was all much the same. I got up
and crept out on to the landing. It was dark. It was freezing.
I tiptoed down the stairs. Creak creak. Shh shh.

I opened the kitchen door, an old door. Flagstones, a fine old wooden table, a settle . . . A settle? There can't be, wrong tradition, wrong house.

Flagstones, an aga (black and dirty cream) which had cracked the wall above it with the heat, a sink, the usual crockery, and I mentioned the table, didn't I, the table upon which lay in the gloom my mother, on her back, I'm almost sure it was she, and my father leaning over, or standing before her.

We were all three of us surprised. But none of us moved.

That is until, after a moment, probably only the briefest of intervals, paused on the threshold, haloed in a faint amber light, I felt I had to do something, so I kept walking in the sleepy fashion of children, eyes vaguely closed – sleepwalking, yes, as if sleepwalking – and went to the large deep sink and filled a striped brown-and-white mug with water.

Very soft water I remember. Tasted almost furry in your mouth, no crispness in the aftertaste. You should have seen what it did to the inside of kettles.

And I stared out the window, drank my fill, put it down, and shuffled back the way I came.

They hadn't moved. Not a muscle. The skirts, the . . . that's not true. My mother's face. I was conscious of her face (for how else did I know it was she). She had turned to watch me as I drank from the cup, and, as I slowly departed, her gaze seemed to follow me out the door.

Perhaps I was proof of the pudding, the *raison d'être* of their union. Perhaps she was as fascinated as I was, in a certain understated way (neither of us let it show, you understand) at this momentary overlap in the family's business.

For all I know my sister was conceived there and then as I shuffled . . .

Did I wear slippers? Are you allowed to wear slippers at that age? All these conjectures. Slippers, feet, shh shh, back to the hall.

What does it matter if I wore slippers?

She may have been alarmed and hoped I wouldn't speak. It could even have been that she looked at me with love, in the midst of love. I'm almost sure she looked at me.

My father stared down, leaning at an angle of about sixty degrees to the floor (and indeed to the table, and to my mother) leaning, looking neither to left nor right, at the point where her face once was.

I was not scarred. It was almost reassuring. Or that's me talking now. It is for me a reassuring memory – that their love for each other, slight as it was, was once abundant, or once overflowed, I mean at least that once, overflowed the boundaries and had to be reckoned in the kitchen.

Why should it matter? Why should it matter that they . . . that there was love? I don't know.

Hatred is an inconstant bedfellow. It leaves you alone when you least deserve it.

It was always my favourite room in the house.

I have not mentioned my sister.

My sister. Little Bea.

Bea. Everybody was . . . She was very pretty. Long black hair – lustrous is the word. And fair skin. She was a shy quiet thing. I don't think I paid too much attention to her at first, she was just something else in the house. But then it became apparent that everybody . . . was better when she was around.

I hardly knew her, that was the . . . truth. I hardly knew her, I was older and I was sent away to school shortly after she was born and I was away at school for much of the year.

That and the fact she was so secretive, even when I was
home. She was always sketching little mysteries, and hiding
the papers when you opened a door. Big smile. Or she'd be
whispering something important to somebody. She must
have been annoying. When I think of it she must have been
incredibly annoying. But perhaps because she did it to
everybody, included everybody in her secrets, you didn't feel
left out. And she had a way of confiding in you that . . .

I can't remember anything she said.

*

I met my wife in Dublin. My future wife. My past wife. She
was from Tipperary, working as a nurse, tum ti tum.
('Where are you from? O really? Do you know the
O'Shaugnessys?' 'No.')

I'd visit her up there when I was supposed to be going to
college, and then go back down the country to work up a
little more self-hatred, a little more loathing for my parents'
way of life, touch them for a little more money.

And eventually – eventually I brought her with me.

She'd been nagging in what was to become her trademark
indirect style about wanting to meet my parents, seeing
where I was a baby, etc., etc. All code for getting
married.

And because she was living on her own in Dublin (in digs
with a horrible lumpen girl from Kells called Noreen) she
thought she was a terrible rebel for courting a black
Protestant. God, you never met a more superstitious sacred-
heart-wielding acolyte of the Church of Rome. There was
no way I was going to marry *her*.

Still, my parents were nagging me about what I was doing
up in Dublin every week if it wasn't my degree, and was I
looking for a job, and she was nagging me about why I had
to keep going back and wouldn't introduce her to my
parents and was I ashamed of her and . . .

So I brought her to Sunday dinner.

Easter Sunday.

*

Easter at Castleowen was always 'an affair'.

Christmases were for selective and confined misery. Easter was for reaching out and sharing it with others.

That particular Easter Sunday began with a flurry of snow on the way back from church and a command to go in and kiss my great-aunt Hilda who was standing in the morning room – 'Go and talk to her.'

Great-Aunt Hilda was, I think, my father's mother's second cousin whose brother had died in the war. She was a short bristly woman who always wore long skirts; these were to hide not merely her unspeakable legs but also her dog Joly – a nasty snapping pug-nosed thing, who had terrible breathing difficulties and eventually died of asthma.

You approached with caution – you approached with *fear*, the crinoline swung, the little beady eyes already glazed with sherry, the dry lips and bristles puckered, you got closer and closer and –

Yep yep yep yep – your ankles were attacked from under the skirts where the pug had been lurking, and you ended up with a pricked face and nipped wet ankles and your heart thumping, like you had run through a wet bramble patch in terror.

Aunt Hilda was a Poor Protestant, of the kind who end up living in your house by mistake. Castleowen had plenty of room, so it seemed reasonable enough that she would come over one Christmas and never leave.

My mother was kind that way, although I think it was kindness born of fear – that of becoming a poor Protestant herself.

'Hildy' was slowly but surely going mad and used to wander the house at night knocking things over. Until the night she got her head caught between the banisters on the landing. She chafed the back of her ears off trying to get out, and she must have given herself mild concussion from the thumping of her skull off the turned mahogany struts – a sound that eventually alerted the rest of us, even my normally comatose father.

Nobody could work out how she got her head in there in the first place. My father used to joke that if he'd known what a good job it did in keeping her put, he'd have had a set installed in her bedroom.

We would have my father and mother, Great-Aunt Hilda –

Who was in mourning because her beloved Joly had snuffled off this mortal coil a week or so earlier. Very funny.

Our cousin Charlie Steele, and his parents, Maud (my mother's sister) and her husband, a solicitor whose name I swear was Normal, though everyone usually called him Norman, and me and Bea.

My sister.

She wore a white dress or cardigan that day, I remember.

We were having lamb.

Charlie, our nasally congested cousin with the catch in his palate – (every time before he spoke, *god*) – 'Bay I have sob lebodade?'

[Mother] 'Sit down, dear, and we'll get you some in a minute.'

[Charlie] 'He's drinking lebodade.'

And so I was.

[Charlie] 'But he's drinking lebodade.'

My father couldn't stand Charlie.

[Father] 'He's not drinking lemonade.'

[Charlie] 'He is.'

[Father] 'He's not, he's drinking . . . piss.'

[Mother] 'O George.'

[Father] 'What? What is it now?'

George. That was my father's name. My name. I hated it.
Still do. *George.* One long-drawn-out vowel sent out to
punish the dragon.

It's one of those rare names you can't shorten – the
diminutive is longer . . . What am I saying – rare names?
George Foley following George Foley. Following another
George Foley, his father, son of another George Foley, who
was the brother of the one who shot a Catholic. Four
George Foleys in a row. Four.

'Do you think,' said Aunt Maud, 'It would be too much
trouble to get him some squash.'

'Who is?' said Great-Aunt Hilda.

[Charlie] 'Lebodade!'

[Great-Aunt Hilda] 'I wouldn't mind, thank you, dear.'

[Mother] 'George, would you fill Hilda's glass.'

[Father] 'God, I'd have a better conversation with my
horse, your bloody wretch of a boy, bad breeding, serves
you right neuhm neuhm neuhm.'

And so the meal would continue, Aunt Hildy deaf as a post,
Maud and Normal sitting glumly, keeping count of the
insults, Charlie eventually shutting up, except for the
extremely irritating snort of spoilt snot every few minutes,
and my mother trying to keep a semblance of order, and the
whole thing seemed to float over Bea's head.

When she was smaller she used to slip off her chair and
under the table. I don't know whether our parents never

noticed or pretended not to notice, but she could spend what seemed like hours down there, while the squabbling would continue unabated back and forth above the mahogany.

[Father] 'You were not related.'

[Mother] 'I was. Pass down the soup plates.'

[Father] 'You were not. He married your mother after your father was dead. That is not a relation. It is predation.'

[Mother] 'It is not, he loved her.'

[Father] 'Neuhm neuhm neuhm.'

The lamb was brought in on a silver platter.

[Mother] 'Look at the beautiful lamb. Thank you, Mary.'

[Mary] 'I had an accident with the potatoes.'

[Mother] 'Never mind, Mary, I'm sure we'll man . . . '

[Father] 'What do you mean, an accident with the potatoes? What bloody accident?'

[Mother] 'Never mind now, George, Mary's taking care of it.'

[Father] 'Well, where are they?'

[Mary] 'They're in the kitchen.'

Suddenly Hilda was up. 'Where's Joly? Where's my Joly?'

Joly was dead, and buried behind the house.

[Mother] 'Sit down, Hilda, sit down.'

[Great-Aunt Hilda] 'Where is he?'

[Father] 'Good Christ.'

[Charlie] 'Woof woof!'

[Mother] 'Charlie. Don't torment her like a good boy, she's grieving.'

[Charlie] 'Woof!'

[Great-Aunt Hilda] 'Joly?'

[Mother] 'Normal, tell him to sit down before George gets . . . '

[Charlie] 'Woof!'

[Father] 'Sit down, damn you!'

[Charlie] (*wailing*)   'Nyeaaaah!'

[Father] 'Get him under control or by god I will.'

[Great-Aunt Hilda] 'Joly!'

[Father] 'He's dead, Hilda. He's dead.'

[Great-Aunt Hilda] 'Dead?'

[Mother] 'Yes, dear. He passed away.'

[Mary] 'Will I bring in the rest of the vegetables?'

[Mother] 'Yes, Mary, that would be a . . . '

[Father] 'They should have been in here an hour ago!'

My mother started carving the lamb.

[Father] 'Good God, woman, you're murdering the animal. Give it here.'

[Mother] 'George.'

[Father] 'Give it here I say. Do it properly.'

He took the lamb and its platter and plonked it down before him, waving the knife in an authoritative way.

[Great-Aunt Hilda] 'Dead?'

'Shh, dear,' said my mother.

[Great-Aunt Hilda] 'Where is he?'

[Father] 'For God's sake.'

[Great-Aunt Hilda] Where's my Joly?'

[Father] 'We're eating him!'

[Mother] 'George!'

[Great-Aunt Hilda] 'Joly!'

[Father] 'Christ – AH!'

He'd cut his finger to the bone in one swift fluid stroke. He grunted, the room was aghast. He reached over for the nearest bandage which happened to be Great-Aunt Hilda's napkin and which she was clutching plaintively before her. ('Give me that.') And proceeded to wrap it around his profusely bleeding finger.

[Mother] 'Are you all right?'

[Father] 'Fine.'

His place was spattered in blood, and the knife was glistening with it. He wiped the blade solemnly on the napkin and resumed carving.

[Father] 'Who's having lamb?'

Bea turned to me and whispered, 'I'm going under the table,' which was . . .

Bea? I am confusing . . . I'm telling the wrong Easter story.

That was the last Easter before . . . It was April or May. Is that early or late? May is late, it can't have been. The apple trees were about to set, or had already set. I don't know – what do I know about apples? It had been an exceptionally mild spring, and then this – a week of sub-zero temperatures. Unbelievably cold and still.

There was no cloud cover, the skies were clear, and the temperature plummeted once the sun had gone. It was wonderful. The ground was iron hard and glittering grey and white. The grass crunched underfoot as you walked. Flowers snapped in your hand.

And then came snow, snow on Easter Sunday. Our last Easter with Bea.

Bea died that autumn, during her first term away at boarding school. Her heart just stopped and she fell down dead, down the stairs as it happened. She was dead before she hit the bottom. They couldn't say why. A defect of some kind, undetected, unsuspected. She had always been private and secretive. And you can't get more secretive than dying at thirteen.

I asked my mother, Why did He take her and not me?

She said, 'He will'.

But that Easter the fires were bright, the skies were clear. There was a flurry of snow coming back from church. And there were no apples that year.

*

But I was talking about my wife and her Easter introduction.

They went to church. I went to the station. It was snowing.

She was nervous, this was her first time at Castleowen.

I don't know why I didn't say anything to her. I don't know if it would have made any difference. In Dublin I had somehow managed to hide my . . . background from her. But when we drove round the final bend in the road and Castleowen came into view – wet unseasonal snow billowing about in the air and slumping on the dark slates – I could still have said something. No, it was too late.

The fact remains that when we rounded the corner and started heading straight for that cold stone hulk, she didn't see it. She couldn't see it. It was too big. And you understand it's not actually that big at all.

As we turned in the gate, she looked out the window with an expression of mild surprise – 'What are we doing here?' The car wheels ratcheted to a halt on the gravel. I turned to her to say something, an apology or something, and she blushed. She had her head down and her cheeks were ablaze.

A nurse! Who had seen bedsores and unspeakable injuries, paralysed by a pile of bricks.

I felt sorry for her.

She had made such an effort to look nice, and I suppose she did look nice, in her way, but it was suddenly not enough. And her embarrassment was as tangible as her breath before her face.

So I said nothing.

Mary came out to greet us. 'Is this your friend?'

My parents were in the morning room pretending to be disinterested.

[Father] 'Who's the little poacher.'

[Mother] 'George, don't.'

[Father] 'I can speak in my own home.'

[Mother] 'Yes, dear.'

[Father] 'I can say what I want in my own house.'

[Mother] 'Everyone, sit down and eat and say nice calm things, you're very welcome.'

We sat down. Great-Aunt Hilda was wiring into the sherry. 'What?'

Who else was there? Aunt Hilda, Charlie . . .

No, Charlie was gone.

Aunt Hilda, Maud and Normal Steele, my mother, father, my wife-to-be and me. That's right.

Normal was talking about banking charges or something and how he'd got them reduced.

Mary arrived from the kitchen, carrying the lamb.

[Mother] 'Thank you, Mary, that looks lovely.'

[Mary] 'I had an accident with the potatoes.'

[Mother] 'Never mind, Mary, I'm sure we'll man —'

[Father] 'What do you mean, an accident with the potatoes? What bloody accident.'

[Mother] 'Calm down, George. Remember the doctor.'

[Father] 'Are you all so bloody incompetent. My own family intent on torturing me.'

My father had fallen from his beloved horse the previous summer. He'd fractured his skull, and they'd had to insert a metal plate. But something else broke in him that fall — his faith in Claudius.

He made a full recovery, but he never rode again.

[Father]    'Good god, woman, you're murdering the animal. Give it here.'

And my mother continued carving the lamb. 'Here, pass that down to your father.' And I passed down his plate, his meat cut into small pieces.

I didn't eat. I hardly spoke. My wife sat and smiled nervously.

They asked about her job and the state of nursing, and about London. They even asked where she was from. And she attempted to answer them. I shall not record her inelegant conversation.

[Father] 'Maud, tell that stupid husband of yours he doesn't know what he's talking about.'

[Mother] 'Carrots?'

[Father] 'He was not your father, he married your mother after your father was dead. That is not a relation.'

[Mother] 'It is. Hilda, would you like some gravy?'

Every so often, they would remember that there was a guest among them and address the space to my right with some banal question, the answer to which they politely ignored. Each question had the air of previous preparation, each interval had the sense of being exactly measured. Each time they turned to her with their pleasant equable voices . . .

Their contempt was palpable. Their manners impeccable. They were effortlessly, casually, ruthlessly rude.

And I thought: How dare you. How dare you show such disrespect, to me, to her. I'm going to show you. I'm going to marry her. I'm going to open a public house in Nenagh and I'm going to fraternize with poachers. I'm going to have fourteen Fenian children who will speak Irish and be educated by nuns, and I'm going to put your name, George Foley, my name, George Foley, in foot-high letters over the door, and you will go down in history as the second-last chapter in a three-hundred-year slow decline from presumptuous ascendancy to selling porter to the fucking natives.

Of course my wife was too stupid to realize she was being insulted. I suppose even then I already hated her. She thought she was doing marvellously well and how nice everyone was. She even worked up the confidence to volunteer an unsolicited contribution of her own, which was a question about the piano – 'Did anyone play?'

[Father] 'Of course nobody plays the stupid thing. We're not a bunch of entertainers.'

To which she laughed. Ha ha ha ha ha.

In retrospect, of course, I should have seen the glitter of covetousness in her eyes.

But it was too late. I'd already made up my mind.

\*

I went to visit her family and got drunk with her father and two of her brothers. We never discussed it, but it was the de facto purchase of my wife, paid for in backslaps and whiskey and pints and stories of cute farmers outwitting the government.

Every weekend I would go up to Dublin, go to Mass with my future ex and then spend a drunken lunch with an enlightened Jesuit from Mater Dei.

The Very Reverend Father Golding S.J. was a most convivial and intelligent man. A complete atheist as far as I could work out – he didn't seem to believe in either God or Protestants. It was really the most enjoyable and interesting education I received and I was sorry when it came to an end. But for the first time I felt I knew what I was doing. It was marvellous.

As the year dragged by, I began to get a bit reckless. When I stayed at home in Castleowen I started going to Mass. O forbidden fruit!

Of course I never let on, and they never asked. I don't know how long they persisted in the belief that I was in bed or went shooting or whatever.

The reason I know the penny finally dropped is that they never came to the wedding.

My wife couldn't figure it out at all.

She thought my parents would accept her over time. She didn't realize it was I who would not accept them.

And when we went down to Castleowen – for Christmas, or Easter, or whatever Stations of the Cross the year is divided into – every time we pushed in the door there was the same empty house, the same horrible air of expectancy, and the casually phrased 'Any news?'

No there wasn't any news, there wasn't going to be any news.

And between that and the eternal argument over *things*, and why we had to leave empty-handed, and wouldn't take even a sideboard for the front room . . .

And no matter that I had married a Catholic, that I had *become* a Catholic, that I hated them, I couldn't escape their constant unspoken hope, their sympathy, their concern, their interfering!

I was a fool to think I could escape, that I could go away, leave it all behind. I was a fool to think I could find faith by abandoning faith. I was a fool to think that if I was too scared to ask for mercy, I could beg a priest to do it for me.

It's not our way, O no. It is not the Protestant way. No, we are alone with our maker. Alone. A solitary voice in the dark.

And so it shall come to pass that your doctrine shall be interpreted literally, for God is nothing if not scrupulous, and your congregation will dwindle to one, a parish of one, *the* solitary voice, superior, lonely, dying, forsaken. And the exhausted clergyman will be travelling ever wider swathes of charming countryside, linking up the ever dwindling attendances and the closures of nicely pointed churches the length and breadth of our land. Amen.

*

Yes, there is nothing so sad as a rural clergyman.

No, that is too harsh.

There is nothing so funny as a rural clergyman.

This one was standing in the graveyard, in the wind, his hair wisping around his head like . . . like my father's used to.

The service was . . . I don't remember anything about the service.

We went outside, crunching the gravel, around the back of the church to the plot.

It was the first time I had been back in St Bartholomew's since . . . I left. I remember the horsehair from the cushions pricking into me.

I remember standing to receive the limp handshakes of mourners, the odd farmer with a proper grip, and teary old men and women, rheumy for their own imminent passing rather than sorry at his.

As they shuffled by, a thin trickle of crepuscular humanity, I remember thinking my father would have approved, it was a good showing, neither too modest nor too extravagant.

I've never said what he looked like, what he resembled.

He looked like . . . me. I suppose. Or more correctly, I look like him. Looked like him. Look like he looked.

I am becoming my father. I don't mean like him, I am actually turning into him. I have his smell. I find his words in my craw, repeating on me like an unpleasant fish supper.

And I remember thinking, I am walking as I so often walked, in his steps, up the aisle, and down again, and I am left standing over his grave, the grave where I first realized I had taken his place. I had become the Foley, la Folie, the first among Foleys. I am the product, the end point of all that evolution and fruitcake.

*

After the funeral we went back to the house. I was stiff and self-conscious because I felt the solemnity of the occasion was . . . I was stiff and self-conscious because I had fallen asleep in the car and developed a crick in my neck. I hadn't spoken at the service. Hadn't wanted to. Hadn't been asked. *Had* been asked, but she hadn't wanted me to. I could see it in her eyes. So we left it at that.

He left me the lot. Everything.

I who had waited all my life, his life, to be disowned, to be free of him.

He had his revenge. He passed it all down.

The house. Its contents. The fields – the Boggy, the Lime, the Six Acres, the Nine. The elms, the crows, the chimneys, the orchard, all of Castleowen, the paintings, the piano, the walls, the silver and my mother.

I was named his sole heir and executor. If my mother was surprised she didn't show it. She just sat and stared at the tassels on the table rug. I thought she'd had a stroke.

The will was read out to us by one Normal Steele. It was very short. The important part was the calculation of death duties – they seemed enormous. Normal couldn't keep a glint of delight out of his eye. Either we sold the house, or we liquidated all shares and assets to pay the bill.

I couldn't sell Castleowen. My mother, where would she go?

But with no money . . .

My mother had become a poor Protestant overnight.

We went for a meal afterwards. Neither of us wanted to eat. Candles guttered, silences hung and gathered like the wax on the table.

[Mother] 'That's a lovely table.'

I told her my wife had left me.

She comforted me, I who have never shown comfort to her.

*

My poor mother.

I met her one afternoon, in town, unexpectedly, among a thin stream of winter shoppers. She smiled at me and her grey-white hair flapped about her ears. You couldn't say I was pleased to see her, but I felt a pang nevertheless, not of remorse exactly, more the warm fickle heat of self-pity, like the sensation of wetting the bed.

I felt as I watched her standing there that this would be exactly how I would imagine a visitation of her spirit in a few years' time. She looked so like a ghost already.

It was cold. There was nothing for it but to stop and kiss her papery cheek. And to hope she wouldn't offer a cup of coffee.

'Would you like a coffee?'

'Of course.'

'Where shall we go. The Metropole?'

'Of course.'

We went through the revolving doors, she doddering before me. I tried to clip her heels with a brisk shove on the quarter-section. The place was crowded and there was an unpleasant woman with fat ringed fingers playing an already interminable medley of Irish classics.

We sat. A pretty waitress came by. I looked up at her name tag with watering eyes. It read Breedge – B R E E D G E – an indecent spelling I'd never come across before. No longer did it hint at copulation, it actually embraced it in a show of orthographic vulgarity.

What's more, I was starting to cook under the arms and between the shoulder blades. Too rich a vest. And because I had declined to take off my heavy wool coat. I had the sense of prickling round my neck and cuffs, like I was a boiled ham.

'Why don't you take off your coat, dear. You look hot.'

'No thank you, Mother. Mama. M'ma. Mamaaa.'

'It's up to you, but if I were in your shoes I'd take it off. Take it off, dear. It's very hot in here.'

'I'm fine.'

'I've taken mine off.'

'Yes, you have. What would you like to drink, Mother. Coffee. Tea. A bucket of gin.'

'I'll have . . . '

'She'll have breakfast tea, and I'll have a whiskey and soda, please. Breedge.'

'Would you like anything to eat,' said the grey-skirted waitress.

I must have displeased her with my familiarity. Perhaps I hadn't prepared for it casually enough. Breedge. Perhaps she thought I was looking at her breasts when I was merely trying to read her name tag with its horrible letters.

'Anything to eat?'

'No, thank you, Breedge. I couldn't help reading your name tag. Unusual. Well, not your name, but the spelling. Unless it's a mistake!'

'I don't think so. So nothing to eat and two teas.'

'No. One tea. One whiskey. And one soda. The former for my mother, the latter for me. And the middle one we'll fight over. Won't we, Ma.'

'Leave the poor girl alone.'

'One tea. One whiskey and soda.'

And she disappeared, silently, but for the sough of her skirt's lining against her stockings, or the stockings against each other, or the gusset on the lining, or the lining against the —

'You shouldn't do that,' came an unpleasantly equable voice.

'What, Mother.'

'Call her by her name like that. They only make them wear those tags to intimidate them. I never read their names. I think it's rude. Anyway, I don't have my glasses. Aren't you hot?'

'I'm not hot.'

I was suffocating.

'Why don't you take it off, dear.'

'Because I don't want to.'

But it didn't matter, she wasn't listening.

That sensation of wetting the bed again. Hot. Prickling.
Sweat behind the ears.

'Take it off, dear.'

'I'm comfortable.'

'Take it off.'

'I don't want to take it off. I don't want to look like I'm
staying. Actually, what time is it?'

'Time?'

'Have you the time? Have you a watch?'

'Watch?'

'Well, it doesn't matter, I'm late. I have to make an urgent
phone call. Excuse me.'

And I left her and lurched out into the foyer. I was bursting
for a piss and was suffocating from the heat, and the cloying
concern, and the overheated piano-tinkling grey-skirting
carpeted hell of it, the hell of it, and I kept walking and
walking and I was suddenly outside clasping the palings and
I was free and I didn't have to endure it any more, it was
cold and dark and I needed my coat now and I could
breathe easily and I strode into the night, along slick winter
streets, out and away from the hotel.

*

I found myself on an unfamiliar road. It had been a street, I
had started out walking a street, but I had kept walking and
it turned magically, primitively, into a country road. It was

like travelling back in time. The buildings began to decay, crumble and dissolve into trees and shrubs and ditches. Fields grew out of the ground and absorbed the asphalt. Lights grew dimmer and less frequent and transformed into birds, branches, clouds . . .

And I found myself slowing, my footsteps dissolving too into the minute scratch of stones on old tarmac, fainter and fainter. Then the swish of shoes on grass.

And there I was. The old gate. My old familiar. The smell was faint but memorable. And there he was. My grey. My dapple-grey Centaur. He was back.

He looked up and trotted over, as if we had never been parted. We knew where we stood. And he walked up to the gate and before I knew it I had opened my hand to reveal a small apple. He took it in one bite, losing half in the grass inside the gate. Horses can be stupid that way. But his breath, his snorting – all the old sounds. He nodded his head.

From around my waist, from under my coat, my coat, I unwound a length of rope that I had knotted into a crude bridle. I dropped it over his head, behind the ears. You are thinking this is implausible. He let me. He let me. He was expecting it. And once the crude halter was on him, I drew his head towards one end of the gate. I have said before he was small. Well, without a gate I still wasn't going to be able to mount him.

And with Centaur parallel to the gate and acquiescent, I stepped up the slats, steadied, stepped over his back, steadied, and sat. He was uncommonly broad. He may not have been very tall, but he was wide in the beam. I don't think I could have balanced on a narrower beast.

I could feel my breath welling up in me in sobs of air, and I breathed. I breathed out the same air I breathed in – an admixture of night, horse dung, sweat and triumph, and the not inconsiderable thrill of horse rustling, I should mention that also.

And I turned the horse's head and we began our voyage. To where? Nowhere, the centre of the field. The ground rose up quite sharply, sloped up to a plateau where you could see the field was vast, sprawling away to one side, rolling so that you couldn't see the end.

Centaur seemed content to walk. We tried trotting. Trotting was more painful. To me at least, and so I let him have it – I kicked my heels. Slightly more vehemently than I intended, for which I apologize all these years later, and after a start of surprise we were off – thundering across the darkness, hissing through the long grass, up a gently rising slope, up and on and on and I don't think I've ever really galloped on a horse before, I was always slightly afraid and disgusted by them, but I had no sense of danger – or rather no fear of falling, danger was the thrill. We galloped and galloped. We knew what we were doing, Claudius and I, and we did it, diddle um diddle um diddle um towards the crest, rising, rising, a dark limit to our horizon, and we were gaining and gaining, and we were there! – and down below the vast field continued in a grand sweep down to a valley, and so did we, galloping, galloping, and I rode Claudius on, urging him on, I who know nothing about horses, galloping bareback, without a saddle, without my father, it was Centaur, not Claudius, not Claudius, saddled, grazing, without a rider, without my father, and the river glittered below and there were hills on the far side, but this was a huge grey field in the grey night with a grey horse and me sailing through it, galloping, galloping, and a house.

A house with lights on in the windows, the only one for miles.

Quite a big house, and it too was in the field.

And we stopped.

I didn't want to go any closer and risk being seen by some angry farmer or someone as mundane. So I cursed him. I

cursed him for his house, for his good fortune, his life in this
valley with an uninterrupted field leading up away out of
sight, and his horse, and –

What was I doing with an apple and a bridle? I don't know
anything about horses. I must have stayed and sat with her
in the hideous hotel. I drank my whiskey and soda and
sweated and bore the fetid despair like a son should. I must
be confusing it with another night. But it happened. I
remember.

Perhaps it was my house. Perhaps it was my house I cursed,
my life in that valley. Perhaps I was going home and that
was the cause for my fury, that I had made it . . . home. And
I did not recognize it.

I am the first of my line, the last of my line, the end of the
line, it all ends with me. I have seen my name, his name, on
our grave.

I can't keep things separate. These people around me, my
childhood, my adulthood, they will not stay put. My father,
my mother, my sister, my . . . wife. They are all gone from
me.

My life, my poor life, I have hastened through it, without
consideration, without regard, now I retrace it silently with
regret. I tread the same old patch of loss and fear.

Do I understand it better now? Do I remember it better
now?

Yesterday I found an old pair of shoes. In a bag, under the
bed. They have holes in the soles and are dusty and creased.
Still they're better than the ones I must have replaced them
with.

I'm wearing them now.

Now I can retrace my steps as I go forth.

*Blackout.*